American Pie
~Slice of Life Essays on America and Japan~

American Pie
~Slice of Life Essays on America and Japan~

Copyright © 2000 Kay Hetherly
ISBN 978-4-14-035057-7 C0082
All rights reserved.
Printed in Japan.

NHK Publishing, Inc.(NHK Shuppan)
https://www.nhk-book.co.jp

No part of this book may be used or reproduced in any manner whatsoever without written permission, except in the case of brief quotations embodied in critical articles and reviews. For information, write to NHK Publishing (NHK Shuppan), 10-3 Udagawa-cho, Shibuya, Tokyo, 150-0042.

Book design by Takeshi Hatanaka
Illustrations by Naomi Okamura
Proofreading by Mariko Kakehi

PREFACE

Mom's Apple Pie

What's the most "Japanese" thing you can imagine? Something that, in a single image, represents the best of Japan? A steaming bowl of rice? An elegant kimono? A breathtaking view of Mt. Fuji? If Americans were asked the same question about their country, they would probably give a variety of answers too, but some would surely say, "Why, apple pie, of course. There's nothing more American than Mom's apple pie!"

In fact, the expression that something is "as American as Mom's apple pie" is known to everyone. It's used to praise something for being good and wholesome. This word "wholesome" may suggest something a little old-fashioned or traditional, but it has a positive meaning. In the case of Mom and apple pie, it's not just the pie that's delicious and wholesome; it's the idea of Mom making it with fresh, healthy apples as an act of love toward her family.

Actually, this may be a rather outdated picture of the American family — Mom, Dad, and a couple of kids are not necessarily the typical family anymore. And besides most people buy their apple pies ready made these days instead of making them at home. But still, even now the image of Mom's apple pie is strong in the American imagination.

So strong, in fact, that the expression "American pie" basically means apple pie, along with all its associations. It may be used to refer back to an earlier, nostalgic period as in Don McLean's famous song. Or to make fun of the way contemporary America has lost its wholesome values, as in the recent movie with the same title. When I chose the title "American Pie" for this book, I was also thinking not only of the wholesome image, but of something larger. Just as apple pie is so completely American, I wanted to try to write about other things that seem to me to be very "American," both in positive and negative ways.

For me, the positive apple pie image of America is not only nostalgia, but still very much alive. It means things like simple country life, quiet Sundays with good friends or family, my grandmother's stories, and, yes, the pleasure of baking and eating homemade pies or bread right from the oven. Wholesome food, good company, simple pleasures: these are some of the things I wanted to write about. But I also wanted to write about some of the things that seem to threaten that vision: the American gun culture, for example, and the tendency to emphasize things like individuality or ambition too much.

I also had in mind the expression "slice of life." It suggests that life, like a pie, is sliced up into lots of small pieces, each representing different experiences. Through these American pie essays, I hoped to be able to show readers slices of my own experiences as an American both in the States and in Japan. In fact, more than anything else, living here in Japan is what has made me aware of the good and not so good in both cultures. And of course, being here is also what has given me the opportunity to write about it, thanks to the people at NHK publishing and all you loyal readers!

Kay Hetherly

Contents

Love It or Leave It *10*

Please, I'd Rather Do It Myself! *14*

Don't Mess with Texas *18*

Question Authority! *22*

I Yam What I Am *27*

Simplify! *31*

A Woman Without a Man . . . *35*

You Are What You Eat *39*

The Less Traveled Road *43*

If You Build It, He Will Come *47*

The Good, the Bad, and the Ugly *51*

You Can't Go Home Again *55*

Finding Chaos in Tokyo *59*

The Good Cowboy *64*

"Taro" CAN Speak English! *68*

Fat Sundays *72*

My Grandmother's Quilt *76*

Something about Summer *80*

How You Play the Game *84*

Bike-A-Thon *88*

Love It or Leave It

When I was a kid, like a lot of little sisters everywhere, I didn't get new clothes very often. Instead I got my big sister's old stuff, her hand-me-downs. I wasn't too happy, but if I complained, my mother inevitably said, "Well, you can take it or leave it." This meant I could accept my sister's old clothes or throw them away, but either way, that was all I was going to get. I should be grateful for what I had and stop complaining. When she said this, I knew the discussion was over.

If you want to use this expression "take it or leave it," just keep in mind it's not very polite. It's used to express impatience or anger toward someone who's complaining about something that you think is good.

There are lots of variations. Imagine this scene between a young couple. They're going out to dinner. She doesn't like what he's wearing. "Couldn't you wear your blue sweater?" she asks. "What's wrong with this one?" he says defensively. "Oh, never mind," she answers. Then they get to the restaurant. She doesn't like his table manners, so she says, "Honey, I really wish you wouldn't talk with food in your mouth." He loses his temper and yells, "Hey, this is me. This is how I dress, and this is how I eat. So take me or leave me!" If she likes this guy, she'll change the subject.

One of the most interesting variations came about in the 1960's. During the Vietnam War, people who supported the war used this slogan against the protesters: "America, love it or leave it." You could see these angry words on bumper stickers and signs all over the country. The message was a very strong one: the protesters were unpatriotic, un-American, and even unwelcome in America.

An image of the American flag was often part of this slogan. It was used, like national flags everywhere, as a symbol of pride in the country and support for the government and its war effort.

The American flag has a lot of power as a symbol. In the past, it wasn't even used as a popular design on T-shirts or bags. At a very young age, I was taught, like most American children, that you must never let the American flag touch the ground. In other words, it should be treated with great respect. Knowing this, the protesters used the flag, as a symbol of the government, to make their protest clear to everyone. Some burned it and others patched holes in their jeans, especially the seat, with material from a flag. In response to "America, love it or leave it," they were basically saying, "America is ours too and we're not leaving."

I wasn't old enough in the 60's to be

active in the anti-war movement. But the slogans and images of that period made a strong impression on me. Even now I feel a little uncomfortable when I see the American flag on clothes or bags. For most Japanese kids and a lot of young Americans, it's simply a popular image of America. But for me, and many others of my generation and older, it can never be quite so simple.

As for the expression, "take it or leave it" and all its variations, they're still alive and well today. The most recent one I saw was on the Internet. On someone's homepage, I saw the words, "Click it or leave it." I'm not sure what it means, but I'm not complaining! ∎

Please, I'd Rather Do It Myself!

What's your favorite classic? If I ask this question, most people will think I'm talking about a famous book or movie. But how about TV commercials? There are some commercials that people never forget, and they even have famous lines that live on and on.

I remember one such commercial from my childhood. It still makes me laugh when I think about it. A woman and her grown daughter are in the kitchen. The daughter is cooking, and the mother is trying to help her. It's obvious that the daughter doesn't want any help, but the mother is just being nice. Finally, the daughter loses her temper. She turns to her mother and says in an angry voice, "Mother, please, I'd rather do it myself!" The mother's face has a shocked and very hurt look.

This is an aspirin commercial. After the daughter yells at her mother, she takes two aspirin, and she feels much better. She's friendly and kind to everyone in her family, including, of course, her mother.

Does this sound like the kind of commercial that would become a classic? Maybe not, because it's so simple. But it's also unforgettable and people loved it.

Why was this commercial so amusing? For one thing, the situation and the acting were exaggerated, which made it funny. But I think the main reason for its popularity was the line "I'd rather do it myself." Haven't we all been in a similar situation before? Somebody is trying to help us and is being very kind, but, actually, we don't want their help. We really want to say, "Please, I'd rather do it myself!", but we can't. If we did it would be rude and we would probably feel guilty. So in this commercial, we can experience the pleasure of someone actually saying what we would like to say but can't. And we don't have to feel guilty!

Sometimes Americans who have lived in Japan a long time find themselves in this kind of situation. We're often treated with great kindness, like important guests in a foreign country. This can be wonderful when you first come to Japan. At least it was for me. My "hosts" did almost everything for me, like finding an apartment and opening a bank account. I was grateful because at the time I couldn't speak Japanese and I needed the help.

But some long-term residents take pride in being able to take care of themselves. After all, "self-reliance" and "independence" are typical American values that many of us are taught from childhood. We may feel uncomfortable if other people try to do too much for us. It feels good to be able to buy your own train ticket, order in a restaurant, or communicate in Japanese. If someone tries to do these things for us, some of us may want to say, "Please, I'd rather do it myself!"

I remember one situation when I felt like this. A friend and I decided to take a taxi together even though we were going different places. When the taxi driver stopped to let her out, she stayed in the taxi and explained to him in detail where I was going. I really wanted to tell him myself! It seems a little silly now when I think of it, but I guess my pride was hurt.

I suppose the next time I find myself in a situation when I feel like saying, "Please! I'd rather do it myself!", I should just take a couple of aspirin, relax, and appreciate the kindness of strangers and friends. ∎

Don't Mess with Texas

I think it's common knowledge that young Japanese women tend to be more fashionable and more feminine than young Americans. Sometimes I really envy them! When I was their age, my typical outfit was jeans, T-shirts, and tennis shoes. If I wore a dress on a rare occasion, my friends and family hardly recognized me! My childhood hero was Scout, the young girl in the movie *To Kill a Mockingbird*, who gets mad when her father tells her she has to wear a dress to school. I didn't even own a pair of high-heel shoes until about 4 years ago. So now sometimes when I see young Japanese women in their pretty dresses, high heels and careful make-up, I think, "Wow, I missed out on being a girl!" And I feel a little sorry.

But I loved my T-shirts at the time, and I was proud of my collection. T-shirts are fun because they express your personality to everybody. For example, you can immediately recognize an environmentalist by their "Save the Rain Forest" shirt or a jazz lover by a picture of Charlie Parker. A lot of Americans wear their T-shirts with pride because they say something about who that person is or wants to be.

Everyone knows the famous "I Love New York" slogan. I guess you could call this a special genre: the "I Love My State" T-shirt. Probably every state in the US has these, and you can learn something about the character of that state and its people by their particular slogans. Texas, my home state, has some interesting examples. One simply says in big, bold letters: "NATIVE TEXAN." The idea is that only people actually born and raised in Texas are "real" Texans. All those folks who come to live there from other states can never be true Texans, no matter how long they stay. Don't ask me what it means to be a "true" Texan! I really don't know, but one thing's for sure, nobody is more proud of their own state than so-called "native" Texans.

My favorite Texas T-shirt is one that says, "DON'T MESS WITH TEXAS." This slogan was started as part of an anti-littering campaign. It means, "Don't throw your trash (mess) on the highways or streets. Keep Texas clean." But this expression actually has a double meaning. Besides the anti-littering message, it also sounds like something an old cowboy might say when he's mad. In other words, "You'd better not bother me. If you do, I'll beat you up or shoot you." This is the tough, John Wayne image of Texas.

Not just cowboy movies, but Texas history also helped to create this tough "don't mess with me" image. Texas is the only state that became a republic with its own president before joining the United States. It was more than 150 years ago, but Texans are still proud of it and their sense that Texas is somehow independent from the rest of the country. In fact a lot of people still fly the Republic of Texas flag, which you can also see on the T-shirt.

Of course, I have a "Don't Mess with Texas" T-shirt. But to tell the truth, my own T-shirt collecting days are over. Wouldn't it be interesting though to get T-shirts from every American state that show the particular character of that state and its people? You could learn about American culture and create a great T-shirt collection at the same time! As for me, I've been wanting to buy that nice dress I saw at the department store the other day. ∎

Question Authority!

In one of my classes, I teach Amy Tan's novel, *The Joy Luck Club*. It's about four Chinese mothers and their American born daughters who often misunderstand each other because of a huge culture gap between them. Though they live in America, the mothers are still very Chinese, and the daughters, who have never even been to China, are very American.

At one point in the novel, an angry mother shouts at her daughter, "Only two kinds of daughters.... Those who are obedient and those who follow their own mind! Only one kind of daughter can live in this house. Obedient daughter!" The daughter's reply:

"Then I wish I wasn't your daughter. I wish you weren't my mother." Obedience to parents comes up again and again in the novel as a traditional Chinese value. And the daughters, just as often, absolutely refuse to obey their parents. I'm always struck by how realistic these American daughters seem.

I'm not sure what makes American kids so rebellious, but the idea that we should "question authority" seems to be everywhere in the culture. In fact, in another of Tan's novels I was reading the other day, one of the characters is wearing a T-shirt with this "Question Authority" slogan on it. "Authority" in this expression means any person or organization with power. It might be a parent, teacher, boss, the government, or just rules in general. To "question" authority means not to trust these people or rules; in other words, to challenge them.

American kids are taught this idea in school. For example, they learn about Henry

David Thoreau, one of the first American writers. His famous essay "Civil Disobedience" explains that it's sometimes necessary to go to jail if the law is wrong. He himself spent the night in jail for refusing to support the Mexican War with his taxes. Another example is *Huckleberry Finn*, the classic novel by Mark Twain. Like Thoreau, Huck breaks the law when he helps Jim, a slave, escape. But Huck doesn't do this to question authority as Thoreau did. He's just a young boy who wants to help someone he cares about. At the same time, Huck believes he's wrong to help a slave because that's what the adults say. But his heart tells him to do it. Of course, the reader knows Huck is right, and in this way, the novel teaches the lesson of trusting our own heart rather than authority.

Once you're aware of this pattern, you can see it all over American culture. In movies, books, TV shows, you name it. So I guess it's not surprising that American kids often believe they're right and adults are wrong. And of course, like Huck, they often are.

But sometimes the "question authority" habit goes too far. I remember one guy in my French class when I was a college student. He was so angry that he couldn't understand French. Every week he raised his hand in class and challenged the teacher: "Why do they say it that way? It doesn't make sense!" he'd shout. Remembering this makes me grateful for my teaching job in Japan! I can't imagine any of my students getting mad at me because English pronunciation or spelling doesn't make sense.

In fact, since coming to Japan, I've probably become more willing to accept authority, at least in small ways. I remember about a year ago, an English friend and I were waiting at a red light. Then we noticed everyone else crossing the street. We looked at each other and laughed. In our own countries, we would never wait at a red light if no cars were coming. We were used to people in Japan waiting, but now we were the only ones following the rule. What happened to questioning authority?! ∎

I Yam What I Am

A friend of mine loves the movie *Casablanca*. Like Bogart, he looks at me with a cool expression, and says, "Here's lookin' at you, kid." Another friend is crazy about the novel *Gone with the Wind*. When she has a bad day, she encourages herself with Scarlett's famous words, "Tomorrow is another day!" One of my favorite lines is not as well-known as these two, but just as memorable. It comes from the novel, *The Invisible Man*, by Ralph Ellison.

Here's the situation: a young African American man leaves the South and moves to New York. He thinks the North is better, and tries to hide his southern roots. One cold night, he's walking around Harlem feeling alone and frustrated. Suddenly he smells something very familiar: hot sweet potatoes or yams, as they're called in the South. An old man is selling South Carolina yams on the street. The young man buys one, takes a bite, and is overwhelmed by homesickness. He remembers his childhood and says to himself, ". . . to hell with being ashamed of what you liked. No more of that for me." Then he buys two more yams and tells the old man proudly, "I yam what I am!"

A variation of the expression "I am what I am," this line implies that your basic character never really changes. It also suggests that where you come from is who you are. For the young man, eating yams and being a poor, black southerner can't be separated. His family ate them all the time because they were cheap and delicious. Buying three yams on the street in Harlem makes it pretty obvious where he's from, but in this scene he remembers the good feelings associated with his southern roots and no longer feels ashamed.

Though my own background is different from that of Ellison's character, I also tried to hide my roots when I moved from Texas to the Northeast at seventeen. Before that, I never thought of myself as a "southerner." And I had no idea that my way of talking was different. Not only the fact that I had a southern accent, but some of the words I used made people laugh or look at me in a strange way. Once I went into a grocery store and asked for a "sack." "A what?" the clerk asked. "You know, a sack. A paper sack," I said. "Oh, you mean a bag," she answered and finally gave me one.

The expression that caused me the most trouble was "y'all." This means "you all," and it's as basic to the southern dialect as bread is to the American diet. Using it up north, though, always made people laugh. "Hey, you must be from down south," they would say. I knew what they really meant was, "You southerners sure sound funny when you talk." Like the character in Ellison's novel, I felt ashamed of my southernness and tried to hide it by speaking more like the people around me.

Now people are often surprised that I'm from Texas. "But you don't have an accent," they say. It's true. I unlearned my southern way of speaking to avoid being made fun of. I don't regret it. It's important to be able to fit into whatever world you find yourself in, and, good or bad, that's harder to do with a southern accent. Still, when I go back to Texas and hear that familiar "y'all" and the slow southern drawl that I love, I know I've come home. I guess I yam what I am after all. ∎

Simplify!

I read an interesting essay by Toshimi Horiuchi about the power of beauty in people's lives. Our busy, high tech lives leave us no time "to appreciate the spiritual beauties which the soul genuinely thirsts for," he writes. Horiuchi's essay reminded me of something in American culture that goes way back: the longing for a simple life in the country.

One of the first Americans to express this ideal was Henry David Thoreau. In *Walden*, he tells the story of why he decided to live in the woods and what his life there was like. *Walden* was published in 1854, long before our high tech age, but even then

Thoreau felt that most people were too busy and out of touch with themselves. "Simplify, simplify!" he tells the reader. Then through his own example, he shows how. He goes to the woods, builds a small house, plants beans, and lives "deliberately." In this way, Thoreau seems to find the kind of spiritual beauty Horiuchi writes of, both within himself and in the natural world around him.

As far back as I can remember, a simple life in the country has been one popular version of the American Dream. In Japanese, "inaka" often has a negative meaning, especially when young people use it. But "the country" is a place many Americans, young and old, long for. Of course plenty of people wouldn't live anywhere except New York, for example, and lots of young Americans, like Japanese, can't wait to leave their small towns and move to the big city. But even so, there's always been a powerful urge for country life in the American consciousness.

American music is full of this urge. From the classic "Home on the Range" to the popular "Country Roads," countless songs express the longing for a country home. One of my favorites is a song by Judy Collins called "Innisfree." In it, the singer goes to a place called "Innisfree," builds a small cabin, plants some beans, listens to the sounds of water and crickets, and finds peace. This song came out in 1971, but the feeling is very close to Thoreau's. In fact, it's based on a poem by W.B. Yeats that was inspired by Thoreau's life in the woods.

This kind of life was also part of my family's dream. When I was thirteen, my parents decided to move about thirty miles outside of Houston. It wasn't exactly Innisfree, but we watched the stars at night, listened to crickets, planted a garden, and ate home baked bread and pies. We still had to go into the city on weekdays for school and work, so we could only feel the peace of country living on the weekends. It wasn't simple enough, and eventually we moved back into Houston. But I remember it as one of the happiest times of growing up.

In fact, within five years, I was back in the country. This time there were no big cities nearby. I spent two years in what I still think is the nicest part of the US: the beautiful green mountains of Vermont. After visiting me there, my sister was hooked too. She now lives in a house she built with the help of her friends, right in the middle of the Maine Woods. She even has beans!

There seems to be something special about living in the country. Maybe, like Thoreau, we know ourselves best when we know nature. Or maybe the power of beauty that Horiuchi writes about is easier to feel when we slow down and simplify our lives. I don't know, but whatever it is, "Oh, give me a home, where the buffalo roam. . . . " ∎

A Woman Without a Man. . .

The other day, a Japanese man asked me a question I've often been asked in Japan: "American men are really kind to women, aren't they?" At first, I wondered why so many people have this impression. Now I realize it's based partly on the "ladies first" idea and partly on the myth in Japan that most American men help with the housework (don't believe that one!). I'm never quite sure how to answer, so I usually laugh and repeat the old cliché that it depends on the person.

Don't get me wrong. I know lots of kind American men. But if you asked women all over America the same question, I doubt you'd get a simple "yes" from anyone. The relationship between the sexes, for better or worse, is just not that simple.

Take the "ladies first" idea, for example. Even if a man wants to follow this custom, he can't be sure how the woman will react. If he opens the door and insists that she go first, she might smile and think, "What a kind man!" But she might give him a dirty look or even tell him she doesn't need a man to open the door for her. Personally, I think opening a door for someone else is a nice gesture. But how about the same custom in cars? You can see this in old movies. The man parks the car, gets out, walks around to the passenger side, and opens the woman's door. And what's she doing all that time? Just sitting there waiting for him to let her out. In this context, the custom seems pretty silly, and it makes the problem easier to understand: for many people, the traditional image of the "lady" and the practice of "ladies first" go along with a belief that women, "the weaker sex," are helpless without men.

There's an old saying that expresses a similar idea: "A woman without a man is like a fish without water." In other words, a fish can't live without water, and a woman can't live without a man. The well-known feminist Gloria Steinem responded to this statement with humor, which is probably more effective than anger. She rewrote it, proclaiming that "A woman without a man is like a fish without a bicycle." Of course, a fish doesn't need a bicycle, and here Steinem suggests a woman doesn't need a man either. Well, I'm sure a lot of people would agree with me that women do need men, men need women, and basically we all need each other to make the world go 'round. (Hey, even Steinem herself shocked the world by getting married recently!) But I like Steinem's humor and hope that both men and women can appreciate it.

It's true though that some women just

don't want to be "ladies" anymore. A recent Hollywood movie shows an interesting example. A woman and three men are being held hostage by a man who seems to be very dangerous. The conversation goes something like this: One male hostage says, "Hey let her go free because she's a woman." The woman gets mad and answers, "I don't want to be freed because I'm a woman. I hate that." It's obvious that times have changed because it's impossible to imagine someone like Marilyn Monroe saying this line.

So you see, it's not so easy to say that American men are kind just because of the ladies first custom. But now I'm really curious. When American men are asked this same question in Japan—"American men are really kind to women, aren't they?"—what kind of answers do they give? ∎

You Are What You Eat

I was talking to an American woman the other day. "I could never move back to the States," she said, "because I can't live without Japanese food." Actually I've had the same thought myself. Japanese food makes me feel good because it's both delicious and healthy, the perfect balance. If the popular saying, "you are what you eat," is true, then what you eat has a powerful effect on who you are. In other words, a good, satisfying diet helps to make a healthy and happy person. I believe it. But it's interesting that Americans and Japanese sometimes have different perceptions of what's "good."

Take bread for example. When I was a kid, everyone ate soft, white bread. "Brown" or whole grain bread was unpopular. In fact, I remember getting a sandwich with half white and half brown bread on an airplane. "Yuck!" I thought, and threw away the brown part.

But in the late 60's and 70's whole grains became popular, and people began to say that white bread was not only tasteless, but also unhealthy. What's good for us is the dark bran that's taken out of bread to make it soft and white. In fact, extra bran is often added to breads and cereals now because it keeps the body working smoothly. You can still get white bread in the States, but these days supermarkets have a huge variety of dark breads because that's what customers want. And not just because they're healthier; most people think they taste better too.

In Tokyo, finding whole wheat bread in the supermarket is no problem, but friends tell me it's considered only "healthy," not tasty.

Almost everybody eats white bread. To me, there's nothing better than homemade whole wheat bread, hot from the oven. The other day I wanted to make some but couldn't find any whole wheat flour. Usually I go to the international market for it, but this time I tried a few department stores: no whole wheat flour. In fact, the Japanese friend I was shopping with didn't even know how to say "whole wheat" in Japanese.

Rice is a similar story. Health-conscious Americans consider brown rice (*genmai*) healthier and more flavorful than white rice. Like whole wheat bread, the bran is not taken out. And like whole wheat flour, you can buy brown rice in just about any grocery store, large or small, in the States. But brown rice seems to have a terrible image in Japan. I was told that it was eaten during war time when white rice was unavailable, and most people still eat it only if they have to. Of course Japanese white rice probably goes best with

Japanese style cooking. But brown rice really is tasty too.

If you don't believe me, I'm not surprised! Most Americans feel the same way about tofu. It has a bad image in the States. Tofu is considered "healthy" but tasteless. Like brown rice for Japanese, most people eat it only if they have to. I hated tofu before coming to Japan, but now it's one of my favorite dishes.

Obviously "good" food has to be perceived as both delicious and healthy. In that way, for me Japanese food is best. Though I love a hot, buttered slice of whole grain bread, "delicious" American foods are too often full of unhealthy fats and calories. Just think about it. If "you are what you eat," which would you rather be: a fat, greasy hamburger or a dish of light, cool tofu? Of course for dessert, I think a little chocolate ice cream would be OK, don't you? ∎

The Less Traveled Road

If you were walking in the woods, and suddenly the path split into two different roads, which one would you choose: the one covered with grass that few people had taken or the cleared one that many others had already walked down? Anyone who has read the poet, Robert Frost, probably recognizes this situation from one of his most famous poems, "The Road Not Taken." After carefully considering both roads, the speaker of the poem chooses the grassy one, or "the one less traveled by." Then he says that this choice "has made all the difference."

Most American school children are

taught this poem, often with a lesson that's actually simpler than the poem itself. The lesson goes something like this: we can have an ordinary life by making the same choices others make or we can have a richer, more satisfying life by taking risks and choosing to be different. Or as the poem says, taking the less traveled road can make all the difference.

"To make the difference" is an expression that always has a positive meaning in English, whether you're talking about something big or small. If a man tells his wife, for example, that marrying her has made all the difference, he's saying that he's very happy he married her. Or in the case of something small, you might say that using honey instead of sugar in a cake recipe makes the difference. In other words, the honey is what makes the cake taste so good. In Frost's poem, of course, saying that the less traveled road has made all the difference suggests that the speaker has made the right choice.

I suppose this poem, and particularly the way it's taught in school, expresses part of the American Dream. That is, the idea that if you have the courage to be different and to follow your own path, life will be more rewarding. It's fairly common for teachers or parents to tell children, "If you believe in yourself, you can do anything: become a doctor, a successful musician, or even the President of the United States. It's up to you." But is it really? How many of us can actually become the President? Or even a successful musician? There are a lot of very talented actors, musicians, and writers in the States who never experience success. And plenty of lawyers and Ph.D.'s who can't find a good job.

Of course, the American Dream sounds good and for some people it works, especially as a type of positive thinking. But it can be a burden too. I remember one friend saying he hated being told he could do anything when he was growing up. He didn't want to be a doctor or the President and being pushed to do something special made him feel guilty for wanting a more ordinary life. After all, some people are happier on the well-worn path.

I think coming to Japan has helped me to appreciate the value of being ordinary. Of course I've met lots of extraordinary people here as well. But it's OK to be ordinary in Japan, even desirable. I was struck by an advertising campaign for beer a few years ago. The ad basically said, this is the beer that ordinary people drink. And that was enough to sell it.

Of course I'll never know for sure which path is better. In coming to Japan, I suppose I chose the less traveled road. And though it has made all the difference, now that I'm here, that ordinary, well-worn path looks awfully good to me at times. But then, life is full of ironies, isn't it? ∎

If You Build It, He Will Come

If you build what, who will come? Amazingly, most Americans probably know the answer. This expression became popular with the publication of a book called *Shoeless Joe* in 1982, which was later made into the movie, *Field of Dreams*. It's a simple, but magical story about baseball and believing in your dreams.

In the novel, an Iowa farmer dreams of seeing the famous hitter Shoeless Joe Jackson play baseball again. Although Joe is already dead, a voice tells the farmer "If you build it, he will come." "It" turns out to be a baseball field, and "he" is Shoeless Joe. Putting all his faith in the dream, the farmer builds a baseball stadium in his corn field and then waits for Shoeless Joe and his team to come. Of course they do.

This expression suggests both the power of baseball and of dreams. It's hard to say exactly why baseball has so much power, but there's no doubt it does. I know when I'm at a Giants game, waiting for Matsui's next home-run and drinking a cold beer, that feels like true happiness to me. And the way Japanese fans cheer for their team keeps my heart racing through the whole game. American games are quiet compared to Japanese ones, but the thrill of watching baseball is the same. I remember feeling it when I was a kid watching the Astros in Houston too. Wherever there's a stadium, people of all ages come. *Shoeless Joe* may be fiction, but it's a dream we can believe in.

There must be a lot of people dreaming these days, because lately this expression from *Shoeless Joe* seems to be everywhere. Just last week, I saw a headline that read, "If you build it, they will come." It was about UFO's, not baseball. A woman in Colorado decided to build a UFO watch tower, hoping UFO's (and tourists) would come. She's probably waiting for them right now.

When I saw that headline, it reminded me of one of my own crazy dreams: to build a sushi shop in Texas. In the world of food, what's more powerful than sushi? It's fresh, delicious, beautiful, and healthy. And these days good sushi doesn't even have to be expensive. Just ask anyone in Japan, Japanese or non-Japanese, what they love to eat most, and the answer is likely to be "sushi." The thrill of eating sushi may be more subtle than that of watching baseball, but it sure makes a lot of people feel happy.

With that thought in mind, I imagined it would be fun to take sushi to Texas. Why not? I could build a small, casual place with a friendly atmosphere and serve top quality sushi. Even bring my own chef from Japan! If I build it, surely they would come, I thought. But after ten years in Japan, I seem to have forgotten how different people back home really are. When I told friends in Texas my idea, they all said something like this: "Don't do it. My God, it's raw fish! We'll get sick. And it's not for people like us. It's for rich people." There's even a TV commercial for an Austin sushi bar that has a white Cadillac in the background. Not my image of sushi at all.

Actually, I still think it would work. Like the Iowa farmer in *Shoeless Joe*, you just have to believe and let the power of the dream take over. Besides, I could put some barbecue beef sushi on the menu, just in case. ∎

The Good, the Bad, and the Ugly

I have a general rule for myself when I choose the films I want to see. If there's a gun in the advertisement, I try to choose something else. As anyone who loves movies knows, this makes it very hard to find something to watch. These days, it seems like 80% or more of movie advertisements have guns in them. So sometimes I break my own rule, and sometimes the movie with guns, to my surprise, turns out to be a good film. But I really can't understand the general public's love affair with guns.

I've never seen Clint Eastwood's classic Western, *The Good, the Bad, and the Ugly*. I'm not crazy about Westerns or Clint Eastwood, and of course it's a gun movie. But I do like the title. It has become a popular expression to describe just about anything, from a person's character, to marriage, to life in general. And it describes American culture as well.

It's common wisdom that living in a foreign country helps you to see the good, bad and ugly of your own country more clearly. That has certainly been true for me, living in Japan. But what has been even more interesting, and sometimes disturbing, is to see which aspects of American culture are imported to and become popular in Japan. Which brings me back to my original subject: guns.

When I first came to Japan ten years ago, I noticed a big difference between American and Japanese TV. In Japanese shows, there were no guns! Week after week, on the Tuesday night suspense drama, victims were strangled, stabbed, or, my favorite, pushed from a high cliff. Popular dramas rarely even showed crime. There might be some bullying, a fist fight, or an occasional knife incident, but the focus tended to be on average people in typical day to day struggles. Not anymore. Nowadays, it seems like every time I turn on the TV, someone has a gun. Of course, society changes and TV has to reflect that change in order to seem realistic, but where are the guns coming from? Gun crimes may be increasing here, but the average person never even sees a gun, which, unfortunately, can't be said of Americans. I'm sure the "gun boom" is not coming only from American culture and movies, but I do think that's a big part of it. I'm afraid that what has been imported to Japan is the stupid American idea that guns are cool.

Guns are not cool. Everyone who comes to Japan loves it for the feeling of safety we have here. If guns become as "cool" here as they are in America, how long can that last? Of course, there are gun laws to protect that safety, but popular culture can have a frightening power that laws can't stop. It's probably naive, but sometimes I imagine what it would be like if youth idols, like Kimura Takuya, decided to use that power to help keep Japan safe. If they stood up to managers and producers and said, "Let's do it without guns," it could have a tremendous impact, I think. And maybe Japan could avoid some of the ugliness of American culture.

Obviously, this idea itself is an American style solution to the problem. Like the American ad campaign against drugs several years ago, I wish Japanese would "just say no" to guns and other bad American imports. After all, there's plenty of good stuff to say "yes" to, if only we can see the difference between the good, the bad, and the ugly. ∎

You Can't Go Home Again

Traveling home to Texas always gives me a funny feeling. Everything is so homey and familiar. Then suddenly something ordinary looks strange. Or I find myself doing things differently from everyone else. What's happened is that while the place is still the same, I'm not the person I used to be. I guess this is something like what Thomas Wolfe talks about in his 1940 novel, *You Can't Go Home Again*. The idea of "home" is not just the place, but who you were when you belonged there. So when you move away, change, and go back, you sense a funny kind of gap.

That's how I felt on a recent trip home.

My first surprise was Texas fashion. It seemed like every person I saw was wearing blue jeans. Even when I went to my friend's office, all the women were in jeans. It was "casual Friday," she said. After that I really started paying attention. We went to a convenience store. Customers, clerks, men, women, children—almost everyone in jeans. The next night, four of us went out for dinner. Some people were dressed up, but I looked around and noticed four men wearing exactly the same thing: jeans and a denim shirt. I'm sure no one else noticed because this is just the way it is.

In fact, I was exactly the same when I lived in Texas. I wore jeans almost every day. I never thought much about it until I moved to Japan. Then I realized that people around me, including my students, were always better dressed than I was, even when I was "dressed up." On a fashion scale of 1 to 10, I would say that, generally speaking, Texans are about a 1 or 2 and Japanese are around a 9 or 10. I also started out as a 1, but am now somewhere around a 4. I'll never be as fashionable as so many Japanese are—I still love my jeans too much. But at least there's a little more variety in my wardrobe now. Still my sense of fashion doesn't really fit either culture. At a wedding, I always feel underdressed in Japan and overdressed in the States.

It's more than just a fashion gap though. During my Texas trip, I found I couldn't give up my "foreign" ways. Like taking my shoes off in the house. How could I possibly walk on my friend's beautiful beige carpet? So while I left my shoes in the kitchen, everyone else kept theirs on. It was a little strange for us all, but something we could laugh about. Going out to dinner gave us something else. We started with one person pouring everyone's first glass of wine. After that, each person poured their own—except me. I waited and waited, wanting more, but not wanting to pour it for myself. Of course I knew it was OK, and even right to pour my own, but somehow I just couldn't do it. Lucky for me, one person who knew a little about Japanese customs realized what was going on. He poured my wine and we all laughed, again, about me turning Japanese.

I like being able to take the best from both American and Japanese culture. I suppose that makes me a bit of a foreigner in both places, but it's always fun to go home and remember who you are and who you once were. Maybe everyone who has left home and gone back knows that feeling: you can always go back to your hometown, but you can never really go back "home" again. ∎

Finding Chaos in Tokyo

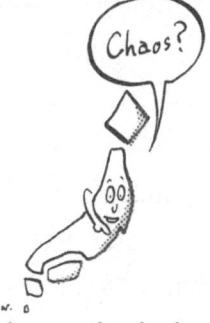

"What do you think about Japan?" This is a question Japanese often ask foreigners, and it's a question I'm interested in too. So when my sister came to visit for the first time last Christmas, I couldn't wait to hear her impressions. Would she like the same things about Japan I liked, or would her experience be totally different?

I should have known it would be different. After all, we never even like the same movies. She likes action thrillers, with lots of surprises, and I prefer a more reflective story that reveals something about "life." In other words, she's attracted to energy and the unpredictable and I'm drawn to order and meaning. I know it's a cliché, but this is how America and Japan seem to be most different too: chaos and order. Some people, like my sister, simply prefer the often chaotic freedom of America to the more predictable and orderly culture of Japan.

This idea hit me strongest when I realized what my sister liked and didn't like about Tokyo. She didn't like the feeling that there were lots of rules to follow, and on top of that, that most people actually followed them. "Why does everyone take off their shoes before going inside?" she wondered. If some people did it because they wanted to, that would be OK, but everyone does it. She noticed that even the guys who worked in the bicycle parking lot wore only slippers inside the tiny guardhouse.

Then there are greetings. I explain to her how people use expressions like *ittekimasu* and *itterasshai*. It's nice to hear these expressions, especially from people in my neighborhood I hardly know or those wonderful guys at the bicycle parking lot. And of course there's *itadakimasu* and *gochisosama*. Almost everyone in Japan follows these same rituals, I tell my sister, so there's always something easy and comfortable you can say. It creates a simple kind of human connection, I explain with great enthusiasm. My sister nods, and looks at me as if I'm crazy.

Greetings are part of the politeness of Japanese culture that so many foreigners love. But then, there are those who don't. Growing up in the South, my sister tells me, she hated all the superficial politeness, the "southern hospitality." The first time she went to New York and saw people yelling at each other in the streets, she thought, "This is great! People saying what they really think rather than always being polite to each other."

So what did my sister like about Tokyo? Well, it's Christmas Eve, so we take some cake to a friend who just happens to be working in Roppongi. Normally, I wouldn't even go there with a foreign visitor because, to me, Roppongi isn't really Japan. But to my surprise this was the Japan my sister had been looking for. The raw energy and crowds of different kinds of people remind her of New York. "Now, this is cosmopolitan," she says with satisfaction. Some other things she liked? The Hachiko intersection in Shibuya when the lights turn green and people scatter madly in all directions. The way pedestrians and people on bicycles compete for space on the swarming sidewalks of Sangenjaya. And finally, the jumble of parked bicycles near the station. In other words, she liked the chaos of Tokyo.

I suppose there's no reason to expect people, even from the same family, to like the same things about Japan. What my sister showed me was there's something here for everyone. So if your foreign visitor won't eat sushi or finds the hot spring water too hot, don't be discouraged! They're sure to find something they like somewhere . . . even if it's not what you expected. ∎

The Good Cowboy

Being from Texas, I often get into conversations with Japanese friends about cowboys and cowboy movies. In fact, I've learned more about Westerns from these conversations than from watching the movies myself. There's my friend's father, for example, who's seen *Stagecoach* (*Ekibasha*) about 100 times and knows most of the dialog by heart. And my colleague who made the story of Shane's pure, unrequited love for another man's wife come alive as he told it over cups of steaming *atsukan*. His passion for the story made me want to rush out and rent the video. And I don't even like Westerns!

Of course you don't have to go back to the classic Westerns to find a great cowboy movie. How about the recent movie *The Horse Whisperer* (*Montana no kaze ni fukarete*) starring Robert Redford? Redford doesn't have a fast gun or ride off alone into the sunset, but he has the traits we love in a cowboy. He's strong and independent, but gentle, good, and, of course, handsome. Now this is my kind of cowboy movie, but it doesn't really matter. Whether you like the classics or a more modern version, one thing is clear: the "romantic" cowboy is a powerful and appealing figure for a lot of people.

Some people are so attracted by the image, they become what's called "drugstore cowboys." In the old days, the drugstore was where young people gathered to meet friends, eat hamburgers, and drink malts. The drugstore cowboy is someone who tries to look like a cowboy to impress his friends at the drugstore. But he's not really a cowboy. He's probably a city boy who's never even been around cows and horses. Drugstore cowboys are everywhere, not just in drugstores and not just in Texas. I've even seen a few in Tokyo!

I guess everyone has their own reasons for being attracted to the cowboy. For some, like the drugstore cowboy, it's the cool look. For others, it's the freedom and adventure of a life on the open plain. And for a lot of people, it's character. The cowboy, the "good" cowboy that is, does what's right. In a simple Western, that could mean getting rid of bad guys and restoring order to a town. But it's often more than that. In Shane's case, for example, it also means riding away from the woman he loves, because she's already married. For Redford, it's helping those in pain, whether they're horses or people. Even if we don't particularly like the story, we do like the man.

Some people say the Japanese samurai is similar to the cowboy, but like the classic Western, I've never had much interest in *jidai geki*. Recently, though, I saw *Ame Agaru*. I can't say I loved the movie, but by the end, I did love the hero. There may be more differences than similarities between the Western and the *jidai geki*, but this hero was a "good cowboy" in every way. Strong, brave, yet gentle, he devoted himself to giving pleasure to those less fortunate or skilled than he was. And on top of that, he truly loved his wife!

I'm glad we don't live in the old world of the cowboy or samurai. For one thing, it's a man's world, and a violent one. But I do like the way these films take abstract ideas like justice, courage, and honor, and make them real through the character of a good man. After all, no matter how much the world changes, what makes a person good is the same whether they live in the Wild West or 21st century Japan. ∎

"Taro" CAN Speak English!

Poor "Taro"! Readers of *The Japan Times* probably know who I'm talking about. "Taro" represents all Japanese school kids who study English for years, yet still can't speak it. Several recent articles have explained why "Taro" can't speak English and what should be done about it. Most people blame the entrance exam system and the way English is taught. While I agree the system needs change, I believe a person's attitude toward English is even more important in whether or not they become a successful speaker.

My own students certainly illustrate this. It's easy to see the difference between the

"Taro's" and good speakers. I always get the feeling that the "Taro's" are either ashamed of speaking English or they think it's a joke. On the other hand, the good speakers sincerely want to communicate. Some are shy, and some are still beginners, but they try even when it feels uncomfortable. By the time they're 2nd or 3rd year students, I can talk with them about almost anything. I really admire these students because I know how hard it is to speak a foreign language, especially at first.

I was lucky to study Japanese in an excellent American university program with native Japanese teachers. We met five days a week and had intensive speaking practice as well as reading and writing. Still, when I tried speaking Japanese outside the classroom, my Japanese friends laughed at my "textbook" style. While they were shouting "maji?" and "umai!", I was saying things like, "Kono osakana wa oishii desu ne!" I gave up before long. My friends' English was much better than my Japanese, and I hated being laughed at.

But I learned a lot from this experience. One thing is that even a good education is not enough. I had to make a lot of effort outside the classroom as well, creating my own opportunities to hear and speak Japanese. And just as important, I had to swallow my pride: I was going to say stupid things. I was going to be laughed at. And I was going to sound fairly unnatural, especially for the first few years. All this was inevitable. But it didn't matter anymore. I decided that learning to speak Japanese was more important than the discomfort I was sure to feel from time to time.

I think good English speakers in Japan have made a similar decision. They know they have to take responsibility for their own learning, and they have to be tough. It isn't easy! Unfortunately, there's a tendency in Japan to treat English speaking as comedy or performance rather than as communication. Just think about TV. People are laughed at for their funny mistakes, and good speakers are laughed at for their "amazing" talent. Even language schools use the "comedy" of speaking English to make hit commercials. But it's not only television. English speakers in Japan are often asked to perform. Someone at a party might say to a native speaker, "Hey, Junko speaks English. Speak English together for us!" Or a guy at the bar tries to make everyone laugh by saying strange things in English to an embarrassed foreigner. This kind of environment surely makes it harder for Japanese to take English seriously as communication. Most people don't like being laughed at, but sometimes we just have to ignore it and forge ahead.

The important thing, it seems to me, is to overcome the feeling that speaking English or any foreign language is unnatural. Make English your own and communicate! Even Taro can do it if he really wants to. ∎

Fat Sundays

I love Sundays. On Sunday mornings I can sleep late, fix a big breakfast for a change, drink lots of coffee, and really relax. But, hey, something's missing! Where's that big, fat Sunday paper that takes hours to read through?

The Sunday paper is a great American tradition. It doesn't matter where you are; every city has a Sunday paper. In a big city, it's about five times the size of the daily paper. Besides the usual politics, business, and sports, you can find human interest stories, book and movie reviews, star interviews, just about anything. And the comics, or "funnies" as we always called them, are great. While you just get one page of black and white comics in the daily paper, on Sunday there's a whole section, and they're in color. In fact there are lots of separate sections for different topics, so everyone in the family can read at the same time. Here's a typical Sunday morning family conversation:

"Hey, Dad. Aren't you finished with the Sports section yet?"

"Not yet. Why don't you read the funnies?"

"I already did. Oh well, give me the Entertainment section. I want to see what movies are playing."

"Honey, did you read the Life Style section? There's a great recipe for barbeque sauce. Let's try it today when we cook those steaks outside."

"Who has section 1? I haven't even seen the front page yet. . . ."

And so on. Of course, nobody reads everything in the Sunday paper, but there's definitely something there for everyone.

Even now some of my best memories of traveling back to Texas include the Sunday paper. My father wakes up first, makes a big pot of coffee and enough toast for ten people, even though it's only the two of us. Then we sit around the kitchen table for hours eating too much toast and jelly, drinking too much coffee, and reading for hours. We talk about politics, local news, movies, or whatever else happens to be in the paper that day. Or I stay at my friend's house out in the country, with her husband and little girl. We take huge mugs of coffee and the newspaper to a big table outside under the trees. Then we sit there all morning, reading and talking. What could be better?

I was shocked the first time I bought a Sunday paper in Japan. "Where's the rest of it?" I wondered. And "What do people do on Sunday morning if they're not reading the newspaper?" Now that I think about it, someone a long time ago must have put a lot of thought into creating the Sunday paper in

America. It's clearly designed for the whole family and for the traditional "day of rest." In Japan, of course, Sunday is also a day of rest, and for a lot of people, a family day as well. But I get the feeling that, generally, Japanese newspapers are written with businessmen in mind. Maybe I'm wrong, but I almost never see young people or women reading a newspaper in public, though I'm sure some read one at home. Anyway, it doesn't seem likely that a fat, Sunday paper will become a family tradition in Japan anytime soon.

I do try to keep up the Sunday morning tradition at my house though: lots of coffee, a big breakfast and my English language newspaper. But somehow I still can't help thinking, "Where's the rest of it??" ∎

My Grandmother's Quilt

I have a beautiful multi-colored patchwork quilt that my grandmother made for me. It's one of my most prized possessions. I know it took many hours of love to make, and I feel that somehow the variety of patterns represents the "patchwork" of my grandmother's life.

But what do we know about our grandparents' lives? Maybe what our parents tell us, or if we're lucky, we hear the stories directly from our grandparents themselves. In my case, I always felt close to my grandmother, but we never talked much about the past. Then about ten years ago, I suddenly wanted to know. I'm not sure why now, but perhaps it's because she was getting old, and I knew that before long, I would never again have a chance to ask her.

I decided to make a tape. It was a hot Texas summer night, and my grandmother and I had gone together to visit her older sister who lived alone in the country. We got comfortable on the front porch, and I turned on the tape recorder. At first we all felt nervous and awkward, but little by little, the stories started to pour out, and the world of small town Texas, along with my grandmother's life, took shape.

Texans are "a breed apart from the rest of the United States," she tells me. Her sister agrees and speaks of the "inner pride" she and other Texans feel. In fact, neither seems to be interested in where our family came from originally in Europe. They only want to know how our ancestors came to Texas. Most Texans, they tell me, came from the deep South, places like Mississippi and Alabama. "Searching for new horizons," they came to claim land in Texas and build a new life. And of course, they remind me, Texas was a republic at one time, between 1836 and 1845. This is what makes us "unique," my grandmother explains; "we still retain that sense of freedom and pride associated with being a republic." No doubt about that. If you go there, you can't miss the Texas Republic flags which still fly all over the state.

How wonderful to love the place you come from, I think. But on the other hand, I know the darker side of Texas history and culture too well to feel only pride. So it's when I hear the next story that I feel truly proud of who my grandmother is. It's a story from the 1940's when she and my grandfather ran a small town cafe. One day a group of soldiers come in to eat, and there's one African American soldier with them. While everyone else sits in the cafe, he goes into the back to eat alone at a small table in the kitchen. That was the custom of the time and nobody challenged it. But my grandmother knew it was wrong, even then. She says she's always felt ashamed for not saying to that soldier, "You go on and sit in the cafe with the rest of them." Again and again, she speaks of her shame and regret, yet I can only admire my grandmother, who like many others, was better than the society she lived in.

Our grandparents' lives are made of a patchwork different from our own, but perhaps the fabric is the same. I like to think so anyway, as I listen on a hot Tokyo summer night, to the familiar voice of my grandmother, telling the stories I love. ■

Something about Summer

Bare-foot freedom...

In his autobiography, Akira Kurosawa writes about the sounds he remembers as a young boy in Tokyo. His list is wonderful, including things like "the tofu seller's bugle," "the monkey trainer's drum," and "the humming of kite strings." There are "happy sounds, lonely sounds, sad sounds and fearful sounds," like the fire-alarm bell which always made him want to hide in his bed. Not only do these sounds bring back boyhood emotions and memories, but also the feeling of particular seasons. As I read Kurosawa's description, the memory of various sounds and sensations from my own childhood come back and fill me with nostalgia.

One of the strangest is the sound of the mosquito truck. Houston had so many mosquitos in the summer that once a week a big, noisy truck would come through the neighborhood. This truck, moving very slowly, sprayed a thick, white fog of mosquito repellent out of a big hose. It's unbelievable to think about it now, but we kids would always get excited when we heard the noise of this truck and run along beside it as it sprayed our street. I can't imagine such a truck now! It seems like something from a horror movie, a poison truck going through the neighborhood, spraying all the innocent children. But I suppose it couldn't have been too bad since I've lived to write about it.

Of course there was the ice cream truck too, surely a more wholesome childhood pleasure. Even if it was too hot to play outside, the cool tinkling bell of the ice cream man, as we called him, never failed to bring us kids out of our houses into the street. With pockets full of nickels and dimes, we would line up to buy different colored pop sickles, snow cones, and ice cream bars. The only problem was trying to eat the ice cream before it melted in the heat. I can remember losing the chocolate coating of my ice cream bar (the best part!) too many times as it melted off onto the sidewalk. But there was nothing better than the taste of that cold ice cream on a hot Texas day.

Another sound that brings back memories of childhood for me is the banging of screen doors. Most older houses in the American South have this kind of door. The frame is a light wood, but the door itself is made of screen to let the wind in and keep the bugs out. A screen door has a kind of coiled wire attached to it so that it closes by itself with a loud bang after you go out. As kids, of course, we were always running in and out of the house, and we never wore shoes. Even now, I can remember how the cool dirt felt between my toes and the intense heat of the pavement that made our feet as tough as leather by summer's end.

While Kurosawa writes about childhood sounds in all the seasons, I realize that in my own memories, it's always summer! That was the time when we kids, free from school for three whole months, created our own world outdoors. Even now, it's the sounds of summer I love best — the ring of baseball bats, the music of wind chimes, the buzz of cicadas, the drumming of warm rain. There's just something about summer and its sounds that brings back that wonderful childhood feeling of barefoot freedom. It's still there, I know, right outside the screen door! ∎

How You Play the Game

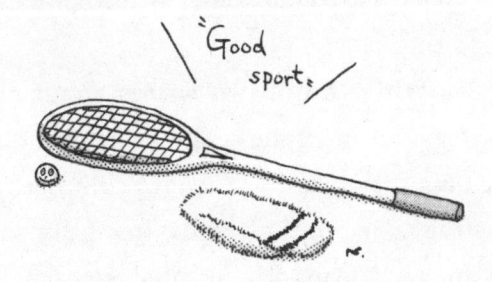

It's never been easy for me to be a "good sport." A "good sport" is someone who doesn't get mad when they lose a game. Someone who keeps trying to do their best even when things aren't going so well. I suppose a good sport is someone who believes, as the popular saying goes, "It's not whether you win or lose, but how you play the game."

When I started playing squash a few years ago, the biggest challenge for me was not the game itself, but my attitude. I literally felt sick if I lost an important game. Or if I started losing half way through, I would feel so discouraged, I would just give up on trying to win.

When I realized playing wasn't fun anymore, I decided I had to work on mental training. I really wanted to become a good sport. I started concentrating more on having a good time and on learning something positive from my mistakes. Like one famous squash player said, "You always learn something, especially when you lose." I also began to learn a lot from watching other people play.

I don't know what Japanese children are taught about mental attitude in sports, but I'm always amazed when I watch good players in Japan play squash. Occasionally someone will yell out or argue with the referee, but generally, Japanese players are fairly quiet and controlled. They seem to concentrate on their technique and fight to the end, even when the score is 0-9. Watching that kind of playing has really inspired me to be a better sport as well.

So the first time I went to the Japan Open, where some of the world's top players come, I experienced extreme culture shock.

Among many of the European and American players, the idea of "the good sport" seemed to have no meaning at all. Both women and men screamed at the referees, used bad language on the court, threw down their rackets when they lost and left the court in anger. I'll never forget one woman who even hit her head against the wall over and over when she missed shots.

I wondered how a person could lose their temper on the court and still play the game well. But to my surprise, the most emotional players often won. In fact, very few of the Japanese players ever make it to the finals. That means the final day of the tournament is quite a display of wild emotions by the mostly European players.

Squash players in Japan often discuss why Japanese players don't win in international tournaments. Is it because squash is still a fairly new sport here? Or could it be that technique is emphasized too much? Maybe squash school coaches expect too much conformity among their students. I can remember my own frustration once when it felt more natural to turn to the left after a shot, but the coach insisted that everyone turn to the right. If players were encouraged to show more passion and individuality on the court, would their personal strength come out more?

I don't know the answers. But what I do know is that, for me, being a good sport feels a lot better than being a bad sport. And my squash heroes are not the ones who win in a great passion, but rather the ones who play the game with dignity and grace, with a fighting spirit up to the last point. That's the kind of "winner" I want to be, especially when I lose. ∎

Bike-A-Thon

Cycle to Break the Cycle.

Sometimes students in my American Culture class complain. They say, "We want to know about the good things in American culture, not the bad things!" But it seems to me that the best things often come from the worst. So you can't talk about one without the other. Take Martin Luther King and the whole Civil Rights Movement, for example. King and all the ordinary people who fought for equality in the 1950's and 60's are heroes because they saw that the society was wrong, and they weren't afraid to say so. They risked their lives to change the world they lived in and make it better. And their story continues to inspire other people to have the same kind of courage.

The fight to make a better world never ends. One of America's greatest strengths is that people are not afraid to criticize their own society in order to change it. Even when the topic is very sensitive, something like racism, gay rights, or child abuse, there's always open discussion and a way to get involved. Last fall when I visited my sister in Maine, I was reminded of how powerful and positive this aspect of American culture is.

One early Saturday morning four of us drove about sixty miles to Portland with our bicycles in the back of the truck. We were going to ride in the "Cycle to Break the Cycle of Domestic Violence." This annual event comes from some pretty dark facts. As we were told in an opening ceremony before the ride, "Every eight seconds, someone in America is the victim of domestic violence." The purpose of the ride is to educate people about this problem and raise money for victims and groups trying to end it.

Here's how the ride works: anyone can join, just show up with a bicycle and register. It costs $10.00 to register plus a $50.00 donation. But many people give more than $50.00. They may also ask friends to sponsor them. That means friends give money to the person riding and that person gives all the money collected as a donation. The people who collect the most money win prizes. After registration everyone lines up on bicycles, listens to a few speeches, and then starts all together on the twenty mile ride.

This was my first time to participate in a big fund-raising event and to cycle with so many people. It's hard to describe the feeling. Of course there's the pleasure of knowing that you're doing something to help others. And the great feeling you get from riding a bike through beautiful scenery on a fall day. But it's much more than that. All along the route volunteers cheered us on and people in cars or standing in their yards waved and encouraged us. On top of that, the police stopped traffic for us and made sure that everyone was safe. It felt like we were doing something important and the whole community seemed to be thanking us. But at the same time, we were really having fun. Like I said, it's hard to describe the feeling, but from the beginning to the end one thing was clear to me: I wanted to do it again!

This type of event is common in the States. There are all kinds of marathons — bike-a-thons walk-a-thons, even bowl-a-thons — to collect money for everything from cancer research to homeless centers. It seems to me a perfect example of turning something dark or sad into something full of hope. ∎

Photograph by Fukiko Sugahara

Kay Hetherly, born and raised in Texas, came to Tokyo in 1991. She has an MA degree from the University of Wisconsin—Madison, and has been teaching American literature and culture in Japan for more than 10 years. For 2 years she appeared as a regular guest on NHK's *Radio Eikaiwa* program. Her future hope is to become active as a translator of contemporary Japanese writing. For fun she likes playing squash, watching movies, and going to *izakayas* and *yakitoriya-sans* all over Tokyo.

American Pie
~Slice of Life Essays on America and Japan~

2000年11月15日	第1刷発行
2025年3月15日	第54刷発行

著者	ケイ・ヘザリ
	©2000 Kay Hetherly
発行者	江口 貴之
発行所	NHK出版
	〒150-0042 東京都渋谷区宇田川町10-3
	電話 0570-009-321（問い合わせ）
	0570-000-321（注文）
	ホームページ　https://www.nhk-book.co.jp
印刷	大日本印刷
製本	藤田製本

定価はカバーに表示してあります。
落丁・乱丁はお取替えいたします。
本書の無断複写（コピー、スキャン、デジタル化など）は、
著作権法上の例外を除き、著作権侵害となります。

Printed in Japan
ISBN 978-4-14-035057-7 C0082

デザイン：畑中猛
イラストレーション：岡村奈穂美
校正：筧万理子

Essays by Kay Hetherly

Tokyo Wonderland
And Other Essays on Life in America and Japan

Kitchen Table Talk
Anything and Everything Essays on America and Japan

Thoughtful episodes, reflections, and surprises drawn from life in both America and Japan. With each essay around 600 words, these are easy and fun books to read.

Can be found or ordered at a bookstore near you.

NHK出版